BLENDED INTO ONE, OUR FAMILY STORY

GOD'S INFLUENCE IN MY LIFE

James A. Newborn

DEDICATION

To my lovely, supportive wife (Tiffany) who shared and contributed immensely to the vision of the contents in this book and to our four children who was the primary focus to become productive citizens in our society. To our fathers, step-fathers, mothers, step-mothers, brothers, step-brothers, sisters and step-sisters…who were an integral part of our original "blended" family from our life experiences with them provided valuable insights…that without it, this book would not be possible…special thanks to Violet A. Newborn who provided the expertise and guidance in the preparation of this book.
God is in control in all ways…

CONTENTS

PREFACE

In our society today, it seems to be the norm to see a variety of "blended" families due to a number of reasons such as divorce, teenage pregnancy which results in a child or children born to unwed mothers and fathers, unexpected deaths of spouses, etc. that causes your "typical" families to break-up…when these situations occurs within the "typical" family the aftermath could result in the creation of a "blended" family which consist of two parents with biological children of their own and united in marriage or co-habitation…the joining of that couple with children evolves into the "blended" family concept that could pose challenges for the parents, children, and siblings. To explore the various aspects of a "blended" family could be similar to the catch phrase "opening a can of worms" due to the various directions that each situation (worm) could lead to once the can is opened, so the primary focus of this book will show how our "blended" family was able to cope and deal with the challenges after the "blended" family was formed in our household. For instance, in our "blended" family situation, both parents had two children each varying in ages from three to fourteen, composing of three boys and one girl. In an attempt to maintain the "typical" family concept, we sought to establish core values (God-fearing, Law-abiding, Responsible, Independent) within our home to hopefully provide the love and stability from both parents to raise responsible adults in our society. We believed that instilling those values within our "blended" family structure would be the key to accomplishing that goal. So, this book will focus on how those values were implemented within our "blended" family settings.

I also included my personal creed (testimony) that explains why I believed in God and how that belief through my life's experience contributed to the insight for our "blended" family. After 17 years, this approach was successful in solidifying our "blended" family into a "typical" family so hopefully other "blended" or "typical" families will implement these core values in their families and be as successful as ours.

God Is In Control In All Ways…

Personal Creed

I have been given the opportunity to put into my own words and explain why I believe in God and His involvement in my life. I believe in God through my personal experiences as a child when I first had thoughts about our world. Let me explain. I remember vividly when I was about 8 years old thinking to myself about who I was and where my brothers and sisters came from and as those thoughts continued…I also questioned the trees, grass, birds, rain, clouds, stars, sun, etc. and my mind continued on that path until I became frighten, but all of a sudden an understanding and peace came over me and from that day on I acknowledge that only God could have created all the things I had questions about, so from my wonderment came peace. Ever since then, I had a yearning to know more about God even before I could read the bible, so I tell everyone now that I believed in God even before I could read the bible. Granted, I was raised in a Southern Baptist household and attended church every Sunday, but I still believed I knew God even before then. There were situations in my personal life that showed me that God is real and in control. I had two traumatic events as a child and two as an adult that shaped my belief in God and my understanding of life at an early age. The first significant event was my father's death one day before my seventh birthday (May 25, 1968) and I knew he died from a life of smoking and drinking plus trying to support and manage two families, so at the young age of 47 years old he died from intestinal cancer. My father was young when he died because he didn't take care of himself but through his death, the two families merged into one "blended" family by way of both mothers vowing to make sure the children stayed connected. This "first-hand" view of unconditional love shown by two widows for their children was a lasting memory for myself and siblings and would set the tone for my future children in a "blended" family.

The second significant event in my life happened when I was nine years old and not really supervised at home, so I was "hard headed". I did what most boys did at that age…hung out in the street and roamed the neighborhood. Well, on one particular summer Saturday morning, I decided to ride through the neighborhood with my cousin and a friend. I had a small "hand me down" bike that was on it last leg but I didn't care because it kept me from walking, so it was all good. We were riding pretty care free that early Saturday morning and were just enjoying the freedom, but it was a day that changed not only my life but my cousin and his friend too. At the ripe old age of nine, there was not too much anyone could tell me as I rode through the neighborhood doing wheelies and racing my cousin, so any thought of cars was an afterthought. Well, we headed down one long narrow street that was perfect for a good bike race, so being the youngest of the three; I got a jump on them and knew I would win the race to the corner of the street. I even made a point of looking back every few bike strokes to see where my competition was…my cousin was hot on my heels, so about maybe a hundred yards from the end of the road that lead into an intersection, I took one last look back to see who was close by and when I turn my head back around…I was lying in a hospital bed looking up into my mother's face. That was all that I remembered. My cousin later told me that I ran my bike into a car crossing the intersection. I didn't feel the hit and was out for an entire day. I was also told that my step-father rode in the ambulance and kept nudging me to make sure I was alive. The joke in my family after the accident was that when I got hit by the car, I lost a few marbles and that's why I was different from my other siblings…LOL! But I know it was God and for reasons only He knew… kept me from being killed by that car.

Those two childhood incidences positively influenced my belief in God and why He has been such an important part of my life.

The following two adult experiences solidified my belief in God. The heart attack I suffered when I was only 43 years old opened my eyes to what life is really about and how things keep going despite what I believe I have control over. As I was lying in the emergency room, on April 6, 2005 observing the hospital technician do this and that to my body, my thoughts were not fear but bewilderment that something was actually wrong with me. I was in complete denial of the seriousness of my condition. I observed my blood pressure rising from 160/112 to 165/116 but felt helpless because I didn't feel sick or tired but when the doctors said that I had to be transported to Portsmouth Naval hospital, I started to sense the seriousness of what was going on. As I rode in the ambulance and watched my wife (Tiffany) following close behind in another car, it was like a dream but I was wide awake. When we finally arrived at the hospital, the doctors finally broke the news that I suffered a heart attack and once again, I was in denial because I didn't fit the normal heart attack victim or at least not in my eyes, I didn't. Later that night, they finally got my blood pressure under control and I laid in bed thinking about how all of this came about…the day before my heart attack, I started having pain or soreness in my throat area that eventually traveled to my chest but I thought it was something ingested or inhaled at work because I handle hazardous waste, so I brushed it off and after work, took my boys to Karate practice, then returned home around 8 p.m., but as soon as I stepped inside the house, I told Tiffany that something didn't feel right, but again, I didn't think it was anything serious, much less a heart attack. Well, after eating dinner and an intimate evening with my lovely Tiffany, I fell asleep but was awaken around 2 a.m. with strong pains in my chest and arms, so I went downstairs and took two extra strength Tylenols with a glass of milk.

I was able to go back to sleep and woke up the next day with a little pain in my chest and arms. I forgot to mention the leg cramp that night while I was showering which was not normal but I brushed it off too. Well, I arrived at work around 7 a.m. and did the usually lifting with the exception of using a dolly to load a drum that weighed almost 800 lbs. on the truck but still ignored the soreness in my chest and arms. As it got closer to lunch time, I was contemplating playing basketball that day because I missed playing Monday and Tuesday, so I went to the gym and played two full court games of basketball despite the pain and during the games I didn't experience any shortness of breath or anything, so I played until I had to go back to work; however, when I went upstairs to the locker room to shower, the pain got worst, but I ignored it and went back to work. When I arrived at work, I put my lunch in the microwave and called Tiffany and told her about the increase pain and that I'll probably go to the hospital when I got off work from my part-time job at the commissary, but after eating lunch, the pain was unbearable and I called Tiffany again and told her I was going to the hospital and asked her to meet me there. She was at Ft Eustis getting medication. I also called my co-worker to let him know I was headed to the emergency room (ER) which probably saved my life. When I arrived at the ER, my co-worker was there and I calmly signed in and was going to take a seat because they were pack, but he insisted that the ER tech check me out first because of the chest and arm pain, so after checking my vitals, they immediately took me back to be checked out. Like I said, my co-worker probably saved my life because if he wasn't there I would have sat and waited my turn, so thank God for him! Now, back to what happened at the naval hospital. The following morning, they did a cauterization on my right groin to see if there were any signs of blockage. I wasn't expecting to hear three arteries were blocked, two were 80 – 90 % and one was 50 – 60 % which is not good, so they had to either perform bypass (open heart) surgery or another cauterization to install a device called a stent. Well, I didn't want the bypass surgery but I also had to trust the doctors and do what was best, so they decided on the stents, which was good but it also meant conducting another cauterization. I was reluctant for another cauterization because the last one was really painful and later I learned that they damage my vein which caused the pain, so I had reason to cry like a baby. LOL! Well, the second cauterization was not as bad as the first and the doctor said the stents implants was successful, so I left that Saturday, only to return the following Thursday for the damage vein, so you know I was getting tired of hospitals by now, after I was released that Saturday, I returned Monday (by doctors' orders) due to an allergic reaction (lips swelled up) from the high blood medication, so they changed the medication and so far, my body adjusted to it. I count my blessing that I survived my heart attack because a military officer had a heart attack while at work the same week I had mine, but he did not survive his heart attack, so I'm blessed to be here.

The last significant experience occurred a few years ago, that really solidified my faith in God when I had an extraordinary experience one evening after receiving disheartening news about my mother and father's health. I just got off the phone with my mother about her heart and kidney problems and my step father Alzheimer's symptoms that seemed to be getting worse. I felt helpless because I just returned from a year remote assignment in Korea and my parents lived in Tennessee and I didn't have the vacation time or money to visit them...I knew their conditions was bad. Well, after I got off the phone I felt helpless and drained from worry, so I went upstairs to our bedroom and lay down next to Tiffany. It wasn't late but I just needed to lie down because I felt the weight of my concerns just sitting on my mind. As I laid on the bed I couldn't relax and kind of went into a meditative state because I was too worry to sleep, so I close my eyes...all of sudden I felt myself being restrained but not by someone on me but restrained by something else...then I experienced the most genuine and awesome feeling of God's presence but I couldn't move....I mean I literally could not raise my body or open my eyes to see but felt God's presence and I knew it was God! It was so powerful but I felt ashamed and was afraid to look at the very bright light but it did not produce heat but it was so powerful and commanding that I knew it was God. It lasted for a few minutes, but I was so convinced that it was God... I woke up and tried to explain it to Tiffany because I knew she must have seen something because she was lying right next to me, but she didn't see anything but thought I was asleep. I told her that if anyone had a gun to my head and asked me if I believed in God, I would tell them yes and wouldn't be afraid to die for what I believed due to that experience. It was one of the most extraordinary experience I have ever had and it solidified my belief in God, because I know I felt God's presence and the peace I had after the experience prepared me to deal with my parent's illness and not be worry about them from that day on, because I know that God is in control in all ways. It's not a day go by that I don't think about my heart attack experience or my extraordinary experience. God is real and active in my life and have shaped who I am as a person, father, husband, brother, and friend. I truly believe that everything happens for a reason and throughout my whole life; my belief is centered on trying to understand and find out more about God and what He has in store for us every day.

"Blended" Family Background

I'm no expert in "blended" families but learned from my own life experiences in a "blended" family growing up in Nashville, Tennessee with four biological brothers and two sisters plus an additional step-brother and two step-sister from the marriage of my mother and my step-father so that was my introduction to "blended" families. Since my biological father died when I was very young, I always seen my step-father as my father, so the transition was not as difficult for me as it was for my older brothers and sister which was evident in some of the problems that occurred between my mom, step-father and us. As I got older and looking back on all the problems that occurred between us, I often ask my step-father "why did he married my mom with six bad ass children?" but he never would say anything but smile and kept providing for us…later, I would echo those same sentiments to myself with my "blended" family and understood that he really loved my mom in the same manner that I love my wife who had two children (not "bad ass", though). So, I had first-hand experience and regardless of the situation, I learned a lot about love, patience, and responsibility from my childhood's "blended" family which provided the framework of how I envisioned our "blended" family.

How We Came To Be

After being married for over 11 years, I got divorced. Soon afterwards, I married my 2nd wife who had two children…a son 14 and a daughter 12. My sons were 7 and 3 years old who lived with their mother in the same city less than 30 minutes from our house, so it was convenient and a major plus in trying to make the whole "blended" family concept work in our household because I could practically see them anytime but mainly every other weekend according to the visitation agreement. My wife and I knew it would be a challenge blending our families together due to the age differences of our children plus not having all of them in the same household 24/7 so we discussed areas of concerns such as ensuring neither parent show any bias towards their biological child or treat one better than the other, not allowing the children to come between us, celebrating birthdays as a family, participating in activities where the whole family showed up for support, eating dinner at the dinner table as much as possible as a family and most importantly, showing love and support for each other. After our discussion, we prayed for guidance to help with those concerns (goals) for our "blended" family to come into existence and be successful. Here are those core values we believed God placed on our hearts and mind…God-fearing, Law-abiding, Independent, Responsible Adults…we were both in agreement and was determined to instill those core values in our home and lifestyle. One of the first things we did was to get them together and explain our purpose for them and the core values we felt God provided for our family. We also let them know that we would love them each the same and no one would be treated better than the other. The glue to ensure the bond of our "blended" family was the love each parent showed for the other parent's children because without showing that unconditional love…it would fall apart. It also had to be communicated daily and had to be consistent which requires a lot of attention to details and the energy to see it through its entirety until the last child was out of the house. We prayed and truly believed those core values would help each of our children become responsible adults in our society. We even had each of them memorize all four core values and often quizzed them without notice…they needed help in the beginning but now each can recite all four of them without any hesitation. The challenge was implementing those core values in our daily lives and activities with the emphasis on both of us being in agreement and consistent. Each of the core values are explained below:

God-fearing

We knew and believe in the teaching of our Christian faith so we attending church regularly and when each of our children reached the age of understanding, we gave them their own personalize Bible, so they could read for themselves and know the teaching of Jesus Christ but we also showed it in our daily lives and before any road trips to Tennessee, my wife would lead us in prayer with everyone holding hands in agreement for a safe trip to and from home. One key element of those long road trips was an opportunity for open discussions about life situations and what was going on with them…it was an excellent environment for those discussion due to being "stuck" in the car…LOL! We lived what we believed because we believed in establishing a personal relationship with God and is the key to the other aspects of your life when it involves dealing with people in our society and treating everyone the way you would like to be treated.

Law-abiding

We emphasized the importance of obeying the law and understanding the consequences of not obeying the law which could lead to incarceration or something worst, so they had a full understanding that if they did anything to break the law, then they would have to deal with the consequences of their actions and if they were in fault, we would not to bail them out.

Independent

We wanted all of them to become independent (stand on their own two feet) and less dependent on us, so we made sure they understood how important working was and establishing good work ethics…when each of them reached the age of 15 years old or older, they worked at the base commissary bagging groceries…some of them worked at the commissary longer (5-7 years) or shorter (1 year or less) than the others but all four bagged groceries while going to school in hopes of teaching them how to manage working and going to school which they might have to do while in college plus it was an opportunity to teach them how to manage their money. All four children were led through the process of opening up a savings/checking account to learn about the banking system, managing their money and even later applying for small credit building loans to help establish their credit. Another aspect for them becoming independent was for each to obtain a driver's license and buying or help buying their own cars so they would not be so dependent of us to take them to school or other various activities. We also assigned tasks at home for each of them so they would know how to take care of themselves i.e. cook, clean, shop, etc. Because the primary goal for each of them was to one day take care of themselves and not be dependent on us (parents). All of those things tied into the last value which was the coverall or icing on the cake…responsible!

<u>Responsible</u>

We knew that we were ultimately responsible for our children's well-being and some of the mistakes they would make; however, when they became adults, the results of their decisions whether good or bad would fall on them…in other words, they would be "responsible" for the consequences of the choices and decision they make in life so we were consistent with making sure they "own up" to their mistakes and for them to fully understand that if they did something to hurt someone, break the law, or anything they would have to be "responsible" for the consequences of that choice or decision and no one else.

<u>Aftermath</u>

We can proudly declare that after 17 years of implementing those core values in our four children. They are productive citizens in our society as of today which is a blessing to our family. The guidance we received from praying about how to raise our children in a "blended" family helped us tremendously.   They all have graduated from high school, two are serving in United States Air Force, one is attending a junior college and one is working for a striving prosperous business. They all are doing well and I believe it's all due to our faith in God and applying the teaching of Jesus in our everyday lives. Like I said before, God have been a part of my life for as long as I can remember and continues to be a very important aspect of our "blended" family. I know there is more to life than what is before our eyes which is invisible to the naked eye, but God is real and I will never deny it…even if you point a gun to my head and threaten to shoot…I will never deny God's existence in my life…I just know God is in control in all ways…

Newborn/Mathis Family 1963
Sitting left: Mary-27 (momma) with baby (Clifferdean-3 mos.), Sitting right: Washington's (42) with me (James-20 mos.) on his knee & Cassandra (3) standing in front
Standing left to right: Walter (6), Howard (5), and Andrew (8)

<u>Newborn/Mathis Family 2013</u>
Left to right: Clifferdean (50), Howard (54), Walter (55),
Andrew (56) James (51), Cassandra (53),

Washington Newborn's Children 2013
Sitting left to right: Washington (56), Cassandra (53), and Howard (54)
Standing left to right: Walter (55), Clifferdean (50), and James (51)

<u>Gleaves Family 1984</u>
Standing left to right: Tiffany (18), Zellena (25),
Janice (Momma) (46), Laronda (23), Jennetta (26)
Front left to right: Zellburge Jr. (14), Kamika (11)
George (12)

Gleaves Family 2012
Left to Right: Jennetta (53), Zellena (51), Laronda (50),
Tiffany (45), Zellburge Jr. (41), George (39), Kamika (38)

<u>Newborn/Gleaves 2009</u>
Left to right: Tiffany (42), James (48)

<u>Newborn/Gleaves Family 1998</u>
Sitting: Tiffany (31) with Christian (3) on knee
Sitting: James (37) standing behind left to right, Maurice
(14), Jarnice (12), Avery (7)

<u>Newborn/Gleaves/Johnson Family 2014</u>
Sitting in Center: James (53) Front sitting: Tiffany (47)
holding left to right: Ji'Mir (20 mos.), Caleb (3), Sitting left:
Christian (18) Standing left to right: Jaleesa (25), Maurice
(29), James (32), Avery (23), Jarnice (28) & pregnant with
(Jia)

FATHERHOOD

When you see a man with a lovely woman and children with them in your neighborhood, the scene brings to mind your father, mother, or family and that's a good thing. I think of Fatherhood when I see that scene play out in my neighborhood. Even though, my biological father passed away when I was very young, I was blessed to have a step-father who became a role model of what a father is supposed to be. He helped my mother raise six hard headed children that was not his biological children, but treated all of them as if they were his own. His positive example always stayed in my mind for what I would eventually experience in my adult life. A few of the lessons, I learned from my step-father, were the key for me graduating from high school and a vocational college, and then enlisting in the Air Force. He always told me to do my best and if I did something, do it right or don't do it at all. When I was about 15 years old, I remember riding with him to help put shingles on a home and as we drove down the highways it seem like it was going to rain, so I remarked, "it's going to rain", but my daddy said, "why did you say that", because to him it was a negative remark, so he immediately told me to stop thinking negative because it could be just clouds passing over, so from that day forward I always try to see the positive things in life, so with his example of what a father should be and the lesson he instilled, prepared for me for Fatherhood. Now, years later, I have my own family and the lesson I learned from my step-father paved the way for my adventures in Fatherhood in which I was well prepared to fulfill. Well, after my first marriage ended in divorce which produced two young sons, I married my present wife (Tiffany) who had a young son and daughter, I found myself in the role of my step-father, but I knew that I would be able to show the same kind of love and guidance to all four of my children as it was shown to me. It was not easy in the beginning but we prayed and was determined to raise our children to be God-fearing, Law-abiding, Independent, Responsible Adults, so we created that atmosphere in our home, by first treating all of them equally and assigning house chores to teach them responsibility, then when they became teenagers, we gave them their own personalized bibles with their names inscribed on it, so they could read it for themselves to learn about God. So, hopefully my sons observed what I've done for them and one day will be good fathers or step-fathers. Fatherhood is not something you are born with, but it's something that I believe God placed on your life. The best part about me being a father is having a loving wife and children to pass on my life lessons.

ABOUT THE AUTHOR

I would be remiss if I failed to mention the one person in my life who unyielding love, devotion, support and dedication to the well-being of myself, our children and our home…is in my opinion the most important person in our "blended" family… from her ability to weather the storm with dealing with me when I demand things to go a certain way in our household that seemed higher than the normal expectancy or problems with the children…she seemed to always steady the ship with her phrase "it is what it is"…which always put everything back in perspective to keep us (our family) a float. She is my wife (Tiffany), companion, lover, friend and mother to our children who have always been both centered and grounded which lead to our longevity. I am the author of this book but she is the co-author in more ways than words could express.

I have read several books in search of the true meaning of God in regard to life on earth because when I look at my life overall, I know that I am here for a reason that surpasses my knowledge but I know I yearn to learn more about who Jesus really was and everything that was written about him especially the missing writings. I read one book called The Gospel of the Holy Twelve by

Gideon Jasper and it was quite different from the four gospels (Matthew, Mark, Luke, & John) but somewhat similar too, so after reading it, I became more curious about how the bible really came about and also, how many other writings about Jesus was out there but not considered to be authentic or legitimate...I feel that we were not given the opportunity to read all of the writings about Jesus to truly form our belief about God. Nevertheless, the life lesson from the bible still influences my daily life in the decision that I make and how I treat people. I have to admit that reading the New Testament from beginning to end during my deployment to Desert Storm (Jan 1991), definitely build up my faith and it was the first time that I ever read the whole New Testament from Matthew to Revelation. In doing so, I was able to really see the life of Jesus in full details
because when I read each of the gospels back to back, it gave a complete account of Jesus life and his teachings. So, I was full of faith by the time the conflict ended. I needed the faith of Job to make it through Desert Storm. There were two bible scriptures (Romans 8:38, 39) that became my favorite from that time and still today.
I live by my motto...God is in control in all ways...jus sayn ☺